Life in the Desert

By Myrl Shireman
Illustrated By John E. Kaufmann

COPYRIGHT © 2006 Mark Twain Media, Inc.

ISBN 1-58037-369-0

Printing No. D04124

Mark Twain Media, Inc., Publishers
Distributed by Carson-Dellosa Publishing Company, Inc.

Level 5: Book 2

Desert Location and Climate

Did you know **deserts** are found in many places around the world? Many are located far inland away from large bodies of water. However, deserts are also found in coastal areas near oceans. Deserts are located near the warm equator and close to the North and South Poles where climates are much colder.

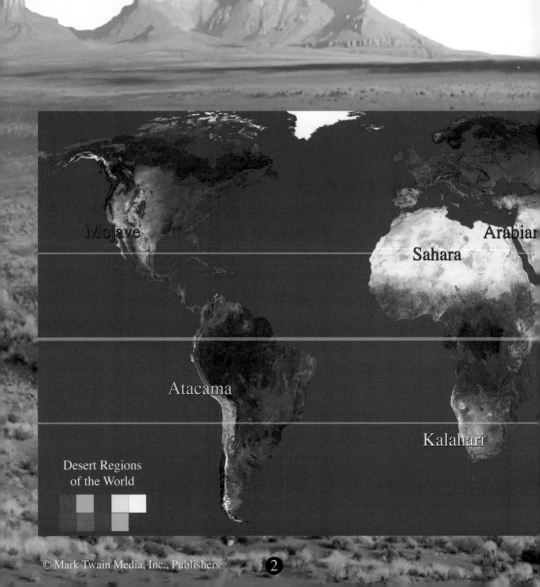

Mojave

Arabian

Sahara

Atacama

Kalahari

Desert Regions
of the World

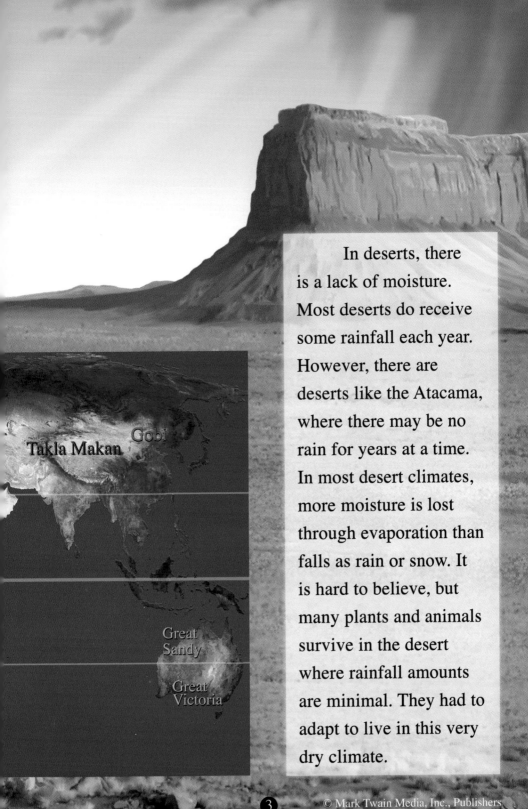

In deserts, there is a lack of moisture. Most deserts do receive some rainfall each year. However, there are deserts like the Atacama, where there may be no rain for years at a time. In most desert climates, more moisture is lost through evaporation than falls as rain or snow. It is hard to believe, but many plants and animals survive in the desert where rainfall amounts are minimal. They had to adapt to live in this very dry climate.

Takla Makan

Gobi

Great Sandy

Great Victoria

You may already know that deserts can be very hot during the day, but did you know that they get very cold at night? Many deserts like the Gobi and the Mojave are in the interior of large landmasses. The **diurnal**, or daily, temperature range can be extreme. Days are very hot, and nights are very cool. The Mojave Desert in the American Southwest and the Gobi Desert in eastern Asia may have day temperatures of 100 degrees. However, these hot days may be followed by freezing temperatures at night.

Mojave Desert

Takla Makan
Desert

Gobi
Desert

What factors cause the great daily temperature range between day and night in deserts? The desert skies are clear. There is little humidity. During the day, the clear, cloudless skies allow the sun's rays to reach the desert, and it becomes very warm. However, at night these same clear skies allow the heat to escape back into space. This brings much cooler nights.

There is great variation in rainfall among deserts. Some deserts may receive less than two inches each year. However, other deserts receive as much as ten inches of rain **annually**, or each year. The rainfall varies a great deal from year to year in desert climates. Therefore, it is not possible to predict the amount of moisture that will be available each year.

Desert Plant Life

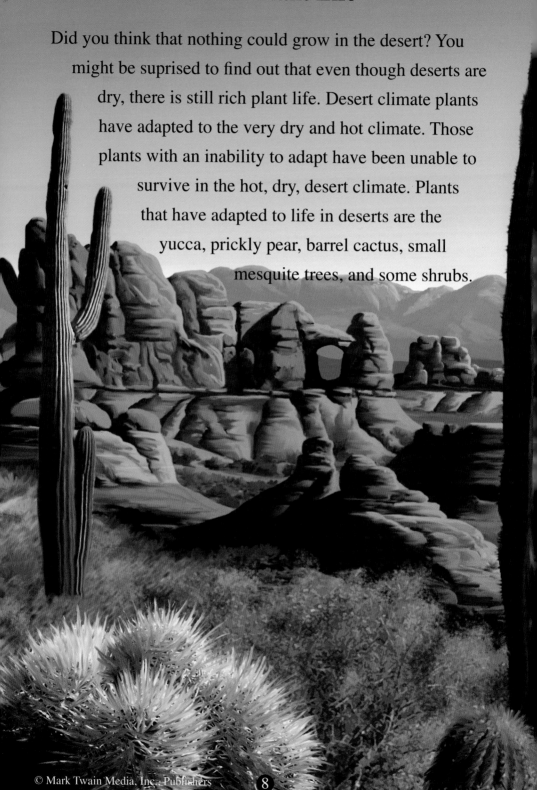

Did you think that nothing could grow in the desert? You might be suprised to find out that even though deserts are dry, there is still rich plant life. Desert climate plants have adapted to the very dry and hot climate. Those plants with an inability to adapt have been unable to survive in the hot, dry, desert climate. Plants that have adapted to life in deserts are the yucca, prickly pear, barrel cactus, small mesquite trees, and some shrubs.

Many of these desert plants grow near the ground. To survive, desert plants conserve water. Cacti have spines rather than broad leaves. Many plants have thick leaves with **cuticle**, a wax-like substance that reduces the loss of water.

Stomata closed during the day and open at night.

There are other ways plants must conserve water to survive because of the lack of rain. In the leaves of most plants are **stomata**, which are openings in the leaves. Through the stomata, **transpiration**, or plant breathing, takes place. In the rain forest, there is a plentiful supply of water, so the stomata open during the day. With desert plants, the stomata open at night so plants can conserve water and survive.

The desert can also be a very beautiful sight. When a rainy period comes, the desert becomes a garden of colorful flowers. Seeds from these desert flowers may lie **dormant**, or inactive, for months or years, waiting for a rainy period. Once the rainy period ends, the plants quickly dry up. The seeds fall to the desert floor to become dormant. There they lie and wait for the next rainy period. Then people can again enjoy the rebirth of the desert flower garden.

Desert Home Life

Many people have chosen to make their homes in the desert. For some, the dry climate is good for their health. However, most people who live in the desert do so because they find the desert plants and landscape very appealing.

The plants and rocks found in the desert are used to landscape yards and make beautiful gardens. The yards and gardens bring great enjoyment to those who choose to live in the desert climates. The plants used for yards and gardens have adapted to the dry, hot, desert climate.

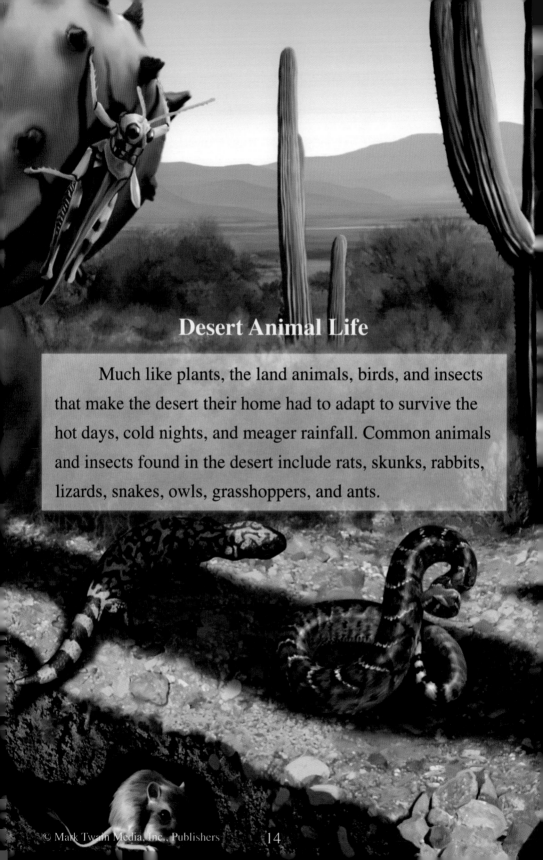

Desert Animal Life

Much like plants, the land animals, birds, and insects that make the desert their home had to adapt to survive the hot days, cold nights, and meager rainfall. Common animals and insects found in the desert include rats, skunks, rabbits, lizards, snakes, owls, grasshoppers, and ants.

Many land animals living in the desert are inactive during the day. Instead of roaming about, these animals and some birds seek protection from the heat by burrowing into the desert soil. Others simply stay in the shade of the low-growing trees, shrubs, and other plants.

When night comes, the animals come out to enjoy the cooler temperatures. The lower night temperatures often result in **dew** forming on the leaves of the plants that grow close to the desert surface. This dew is for many animals a primary source of water that ensures that they survive. Adaptations to conserve water have made it possible for land animals, birds, and insects to survive in the desert.